THE PORTAGE POETRY SERIES

Series Titles

The Body Is Burden and Delight
Sharon White

Bone Country
Linda Nemec Foster

Not Just the Fire
R.B. Simon

Monarch
Heather Bourbeau

The Walk to Cefalù
Lynne Viti

The Found Object Imagines a Life: New and Selected Poems
Mary Catherine Harper

Naming the Ghost
Emily Hockaday

Mourning
Dokubo Melford Goodhead

Messengers of the Gods: New and Selected Poems
Kathryn Gahl

After the 8-Ball
Colleen Alles

Careful Cartography
Devon Bohm

Broken On the Wheel
Barbara Costas-Biggs

Sparks and Disperses
Cathleen Cohen

Holding My Selves Together: New and Selected Poems
Margaret Rozga

Lost and Found Departments
Heather Dubrow

Marginal Notes
Alfonso Brezmes

The Almost-Children
Cassondra Windwalker

Meditations of a Beast
Kristine Ong Muslim

Praise for
The Body Is Burden and Delight

"First, Sharon White finds a mystical space, the top of the world, where there is snow, a mountain village, icy running water. Then she populates it. The inhabitants are mystical like the birds and animals. Sunlight but it doesn't warm. Even someone doing ordinary housework has the flare of a goddess: 'if there's a bed there's a woman making the bed/ solitary/ shaking the coverlet out like snow on the mountain,' 'sun blazing through curtains/ like a fiery knife.' This is a book filled with wit and wonder, 'how,' White says, 'the Arctic must be melting, from the bottom up,' with all that moves under the ice of knowing."

—Elaine Terranova
author of *The Diamond Cutter's Daughter* and *Dollhouse*

"From the start, Sharon White's *The Body Is Burden and Delight* is snug and seasonal in satisfying specificity, earth full with nouns we want to pick and hold, sense and perspective mingle and trade places. Part travelogue, monograph, folk fiction, lyrical narrative, memoir— in *The Body Is Burden and Delight*, the reader is not only bound but encouraged to 'get lost in colors...pots of bulbs on the sidewalk. Lanterns with burning candles. Little suns.' I think of Rilke, Neruda, Heaney. You can't stay away from that, because of where the subjects take you—from inner life to the shared world. More seasoned than vignettes, *The Body Is Burden and Delight* is body and all its elements traveling at the speed of light and orienting on the compass of a word—to make every poet jealous, or to generously give us a guide by which to climb the lattice of details and yearning."

—Peter Money
author of *American Drone: New and Select Poems*

"How does Sharon White manage to make everything seem so new, so freshly swept inside and out, and at the same time so ancient, primeval, raw—the world as it was before the first footprint? You can find yourself anywhere on earth in this book, and the message is the same. The landscape has its own story. This poet takes on the powers of Eve to rewild all of it."

—Karen Donovan
author of *Monad+Monadnock*

"Wherever you are in Sharon White's poems—inside a Japanese garden or beside a river in Vilnius or bordering a reindeer run in Lapland—you always know what you are becoming: human at the point of utterance, young and aging and mythic and ghostly. Her inventiveness edges spring blooms and blue snow with whispering cruelties: a remembered 'long thin face' and a carpenter bee's 'miniature dune' of sawdust, seven cedar waxwings killed for pecking a poor man's strawberries. Read this book all at once and then linger over her icy, wise language line by line. I keep repeating the word 'wonder' when I think about her work."

—Eli Goldblatt
author of *For Instance* and *Wissahickon Creek: Walks & Dreams*

"In these poems, Sharon White invites us to the elemental edges of our world—not to Stockholm or Oslo, Glasgow or Cardiff, but to Saadteskenjuana, Hirsholm, Llanfrothen, St. Ninian's Isle. Here, the observer finds 'no boundaries between sky and sea, land and lamb, bird and call'; and 'even you too have no boundary' in the scouring wind, rough seas, roar of snowmelt, rising mist, shimmery light: 'It's so easy to slip from one world to the next.' As I read this work, I'm swept away by White's exquisite evocations of these various landscapes; I'm drawn into the radical self-forgetfulness she poses for us. But in all this entrancing beauty, White doesn't let us side-step the people who inhabit these spaces so precariously—the women who shoulder responsibility, the boys proud of achievement, the isolated artists, the ghosts. Finding herself in Vilnius, where her grandmother was killed, where her mother began her own precarious journey towards safety, White's speaker registers with irony the misleading messages we might choose to take from the natural world: 'the sky was pure blue. Innocent, benign, all those words that meant one is not responsible for anything.' Ah, this book insists, but we are."

—Nathalie Anderson
author of *Stain*

"The poems in *The Body Is Burden and Delight* are wrested from sacred places, gathered from lives and landscapes that the traveling poet has made her own through the precision of her craft and the lyric intensity of her vision. Sharon White conjures runic wisdom in language fresh as an open wound: these poems are blood on snow, tracks across wilderness, wild wonder at life's violence and beauty, its promises and costs. No other contemporary poet has so successfully melded experience and yearning, landscape and psyche, as White does in this book. Whether written in Anglo-Saxon half-lines, riddles, unrhymed couplets, or her exquisite prose, these poems are the fruit of a life of learning, a love of language, and a sustained inquiry into the nature of personhood. White has traveled the world, but she is not a world-traveling poet, she is a world poet."

—Richard Hoffman
author of *Noon until Night*

THE BODY

is

BURDEN

and

DELIGHT

SHARON WHITE

Cornerstone Press
Stevens Point, Wisconsin

Cornerstone Press, Stevens Point, Wisconsin 54481
Copyright © 2023 Sharon White
www.uwsp.edu/cornerstone

Printed in the United States of America by
Point Print and Design Studio, Stevens Point, Wisconsin

Library of Congress Control Number: 2022947738
ISBN: 979-8-9869663-2-8

Excerpts from "Higher Than All Mountains" as translated by Harald Gaski, copyright © 1998 by Harald Gaski. Used by permission of the author. All rights reserved.

Cornerstone Press titles are produced in courses and internships offered by the Department of English at the University of Wisconsin–Stevens Point.

DIRECTOR & PUBLISHER   EXECUTIVE EDITOR
Dr. Ross K. Tangedal   Jeff Snowbarger

SENIOR EDITORS
Lexie Neeley, Monica Swinick, Kala Buttke

PRESS STAFF
Grace Dahl, Patrick Fogarty, Angela Green, Cal Henkens, Brett Hill, Ryan Jensen, Julia Kaufman, Hunter Kiesow, Amanda Leibham, Maria Scherer, Abbi Wasielewski

For Scott

Also by Sharon White:

FICTION
Boiling Lake (On Voyage)

POETRY
Eve & Her Apple
Bone House

NONFICTION
Vanished Gardens: Finding Nature in Philadelphia
Field Notes, A Geography of Mourning

Contents

Spring

Spring Migration 3

If There's a Dish There's a Woman 6

Everything is Liquid 8

The Weaving Shed 10

What You Do 14

Spring Night 15

On Hirsholmene 16

Simmer Dim

St Ninian's Isle 23

The Body Is Burden and Delight 24

Bags of Wool 29

Island Blues 30

Light 35

Quince 36

The Path at Llanfrothen 37

The Italian Mystery 39

Owl-light

Snow 45

Letter 46

Imitating Celestial Things 47

Late Snow 57

When the Child Was Born 59

In the Shed 60

The Forest Near Paneriai 62

Water 65

Notes 67

Acknowledgments 69

Spring

It is hard to make progress barefoot.
Nothing is built by talk alone.

The father on the verge of being born
the son already running in the woods.

Spring Migration

Near Emma Ricklund's Summer House

Surprised by farms, piles of birchwood and pine on the bus north
  black rivers cut woods swollen with snowmelt and rain, the sticky
    leaves of birches, a boy holding a bag of cookies,
  butter staining brown paper, cap pulled low over his eyes
matted yellow grasses, red
    (wooden)
houses silent yards moving in permanent twilight north,
  reindeer running along the tracks
      small, white, and brown in a cluster
    (and the animal who'll kill a reindeer
even if it's not hungry)
      when we stop, there's a boy with a reindeer dog,
"She's young, a bit unsteady," he says, "my first dog, I'm not
      sure she'll be good"

In Saxnas, spring snow (corn), frozen hard enough to walk on
    heather, bayberry, green furry haze of poppies, tiny yellow bells
on the lake, little bird with dark head, white breast
  at the store I meet a man who says he doesn't like sweets
    in the hospital (with cancer) they gave him sweet things for
breakfast
    "I'm back now," he tells me
  3 large reindeer on the slope below the house
fuzzy brown horns, cream and

                                                brown coats
take off down the road, heads held high, loping away
    hollow hair, like string, white, stiff, tough

A boy getting a ride to the church village says,
    "my mother broke with my father and she married Jorgen,
        very nice here, the people trees birds
Have you been to Hollywood? Is it crowded?"
    (The key to the church heavy, brown,
    rough in the palm of my hand)

    reindeer come through the place where the mountain
    rests like a boat on the ground
people lumbered here to get to America (or Saxnas) huddled
                        under scratchy branches their first year
(black bears eat the reindeer calves)

Everything's ready to burst
buds, slim shoots, purple weeds, fat leaves crawling
    ancient lichen gray-green swallowing sun on chunks of rocks
    I walk out to an island
reindeer tracks in the snow
    time exploded (a star), all gathered—layered waiting
(Emma's husband Folke had a child with a nurse and then left her
    and then had another child

Lisa's lover (Emma's uncle) had four children
    with four other women, she lived alone in
        a little red

house Folke built her—)

Emma had a garden (orange poppies)

—a sparkly quilt she made for their bed—

but (when

they

divorced) she slept in a little room on the third floor

(in a narrow bed)

a round window looking out

at lake and mountains

Roar of snowmelt in all the streams & rivers & rivulets & trickles

—bathed in sunlight—

echoes

the twitter/chatter of birds—(and now a truck)

(& now a carpenter bee)

Saxnas

If There's a Dish There's a Woman

washing the dish,
>   sprinkled with flowers

a towel in her hands as she dries
>   the dish

if there's a bed there's a woman
>   making the bed—solitary—shaking the

coverlet out
>   like snow on the mountains

if there's a floor there's a girl
>   mopping, mopping—

wiping her brow with her slim hand
>   her skirt moving like water along the floor

if there's a clothesline
>   there's a mother, wrapping her

hands around the wet legs of her
>   son's jeans, the sodden torso of his

>   shirt
windy—all will dry soon

a sink filled with water and
>   yes, a woman dipping her hands into the

suds, bringing pots up one by
>   one like treasure,

until they gleam copper

the sun's high
        there's no night

reindeer calving
        on frozen slopes

Sun blazes through curtains
        like a fiery knife until she opens the window

and welcomes the air
        soft, cool

if there's a chimney, smoke hoots its way
        curled like lichen

the smell
        keeping her company as she

sits by the hearth

Ricklundgarden

Everything is Liquid

Flute songs of hidden birds

                 hoot of the owl

the parables of the man in yellow pushing the wheelbarrow

        (filled with birch logs)

            all the twigs expectant

                the lake though half frozen

oozes with light

        midnight dissolving

pink and gold

        liquid curtains

spilled into the mind

        liquid too with all this spring

so much light

        swallowed whole

by furry muzzle/ metallic beak

            unnecessary

invasive

        the telegraph of birds

morning hatches

        like syrup

sweet and

        (celestial)

        lake breaking up

susurration

snow/ice building along the ragged

shore
    then the knife cut
        all rushing toward Saxnas
(black and blue surface)
    reindeer moving up
           the mountain to calve
    even though there's nothing to eat
(and they're starving)

Kultsjon

The Weaving Shed

1

Kittiwakes, fulmar, common terns, Arctic terns waiting on the shingle. Piles of cinnamon kelp at their feet. It's hard to explain what it is about the gannets that's like another universe. Not shaped like any birds I know, and they fly.

The air part of their feathers. They can't get too close in their apartments on the cliff: Their beaks so sharp they'd slice each other up.

All I can see suspended above the road is ocean. Not quite right, the ocean hot on the stones, pasture with tiny pink orchids, hills overlapping in green and not quite ripe heather. Beyond the frame of the window are the birds. No boundaries between sky and sea, land and lamb, bird and call. The lark catapults into the sky much higher than you can imagine, filled with song—skylark—her name defines her. The oystercatcher puts her nest right on the road to Hillswick, woven of long grass, her speckled eggs patient, trusting the workers won't smash the life out of them. Even you too have no boundary, air pushing all the things you knew as skin, teeth, eyelids away, so the body is only really part of everything else, shell-like, gone when the oystercatcher splits us in two, discards whatever isn't food.

The house is a cave, peat burning at the center. Kettle hung over the fire. Outside, wind refuses to go away. Stones cracking on the cliffs, thrown up in raw chunks, a giant's game. But I love it here, the lambs a comfort in the dark light. Their faces lined up as the years go by, one more perfect than the next. The sea breaks over and over, frantic, then not frantic at all.

Isn't it like that to play golf, one ball after another, having a bash at the ball. The curving idea of the links, course running above the burn. Interesting the river is a burn. Hot, vital, a way to reach the giant's stones on the way to the waterfall.

2.

An orange buoy takes up a spot in the foreground just waiting for a boat. And what does the boat say? Hard to tell, some things are untranslatable. The body entangled. Is death just the release of that bright spark? What about the seal, not quite here, born too soon, no mother in sight. It seems worth it to give her that chance to live.

Not pretty, not pretty at all, but miraculous, each iteration of the form, orchid bright, seal eye, wave something entirely different from what it was the day before. Riled up, capable of violence. Think about the tsunami, lifting whole cities off their feet and crashing down somewhere else, splinters of the world shaken.

Wind batters the side of the weaving shed. Nothing new in that. It's a mini gale.

I've been trying to think about Danish artist Emilie Demant Hatt here. Her paintings after her time on these far islands. I remember one about ghosts, four women by the cliff, a gash like the ones on the ness, very dark. Not the time when seabirds nest, but winter, much less light. The women's heads are bowed, they stare down into the frothing water, popping up like a geyser into the air. I want to get back to light. Illumination. And how so many things are working hard to diminish this free gift.

Northern divers, two in the bay. Perfectly calm, but the shimmer's there. The sound of wings, even the kids at school recognize birds by their sound. If I'm filled with light, what happens then?

3.

Each night I think I might be forgetting everything. Or at least that's what my dreams tell me. My purse on the grocery cart. The clothes I bought in a plastic bag. A house I never lived in, the sound of anyone's voice. Mother, father, the bark of all the dogs I've loved. An accounting of buttons, some for the wool trade, resin capturing shells picked up on beaches, tiny iridescent whorls of light, light the underside of clouds.

We think the otter licked the butter wrapper last night. We think the white van is a rape van, but it isn't. We think the van on the hill near the manure dump is a caravan, but it isn't. It's just someone fixing the fences. We saw him later by the roadside near the chambered cairn, unloading a roll of fence from his truck.

We think the oystercatchers are quiet for once, but they aren't, chasing me in bands of six or seven along the black rocks by the shore. I think the piled up rocks covered with hairy lichen are so old, but they aren't, really, only one or two centuries ago before the fishing stopped or the laird kicked the crofters off his land and replaced them with sheep. Whole villages disappeared in a wink. We float on the world here. You can't turn anywhere without day seeping under your feathers. Everyone feels it. The kids whisper they can't wait till the summer break. They're all tired. Too much daylight.

One boy tells me he loves to drive the tractor, baling silage with his father. And then he shows me his painting of a killer whale. He unfolds the parts slowly and holds it up for me to see. It's to scale, he says.

4.

I think the eye is just a piece of the soul. I think I don't really have a soul at all. Just a mechanical body attached to something that wants. Wants the tern to keep on flying and muttering and caring. Wants the apples to have a tree, the gospel to have a text, the priest to stop whining. The stones to keep up the good work all over the island, singing praises to the sea on one side, the ocean on another, wants the light, the light of the north to keep on infusing us all with this energy that won't go away, wants the piano to let me sing on her keys, the sparkling water to do its magic back and forth back and forth on the margins of the beach, now strewn with stones.

5.

I don't miss trees. Or the conversation of experts in the paper. Conversation of neighbors in the streets. I don't miss the boom of trucks or laughter of drunks outside my window. I like to be swept clean. Though I'm not. Everything harried is erased for a moment. The ocean pulls out kelp and then puts it back on the sand. All the birds I can't name stand up and watch the wind. They've gone now, off to calm seas.

I'm very old and then I'm not. My heart knitted and knot for no reason. I refuse to tick off the years like treasure. If I refuse to name time, does that absolve me from all this? Who knows? The ginger cake is the best here.

Hillswick

What You Do

Slice the trees into pieces
                Pile their twig fingers near the shed
Measure stones for a path
                Straight and narrow to the
Small red house
                Listen to the wind, dismiss it
Rake the grass already blushing
                                new green
Build two tiny outhouses
                Stained with wind
Wish you lived somewhere else
                                By a warm sea
Dark nights
                Beautiful women who'd talk to you
With their eyes
                your arm
Held mute by your side
                As the wind pulls up the
Tips of your hair
                Wear your boots when it's wet,
Moss sinks under
                The shiny water
Polish the feet of the trees
                All night that's no night
But the burning eye of spring

Saadteskenjuana

Spring Night

Is memory
       like the uncertain touch
past noon

though winds blow
       in the dim light
red and red

since I was suddenly
       sent away—
the hours of the spring night

are short
       these dream meetings
on peaks before, peaks behind
       snow glistening
white

no fixed lodgings
       coming and going
submit to you

I came to this spring field
       to pick violets
but I loved the field
       so

in the dim light red and red
       your sisters all must
stay at home

On Hirsholmene

for Emilie Demant Hatt

Sometimes I think I can run my fingers on the tops of tables. Lick butter, spin light here like cloth. Some things never leave me. And some things do. The island's amusing. So many birds. The dark black velvet of their wings. There's a caretaker with a boat. Funny, laughing. All bluster but sweet. Parks his cart on the dock till he's needed. Empty most of the time. No one brings anything. It's useless—happiness floats off the surface of the sea like perfume. So many blues, so many twists of white on the seabirds' wings. So many rounded stones, piled up along the fields. It's so easy to slip from one world to the next.

The caretaker's wife's in her garden planting tiny seeds in salty soil. Mud dark. The sea's navy blue. Really. She's robed in red. Her husband reminds me of the old wolf. All bent and busy. Putting the oars on the top of the stone wall. Red. So many things I loved were red. Red hat, red trim. Red sky. Red skirt. The line of reindeer, pulling red sleds. Whatever. Doesn't matter now. Light is what matters. How light fills the heart.

What if, she thought, there was more to the world than sun, sea, moon, field. The little fields around her bordered by rocks. She knew it wasn't far from the place where Carl and Anne Marie spent weeks in the summer. Was she just old, not dead? Just old, and wanting so much to remember the taste of his tongue on hers? The birds fly by with rustling wings. The terns fly a dance near the horizon. Each matches the other in the air.

The man who she loved was Gudmund. She knew that now. Loved birds, too. They brought a dove back from St. Thomas. A smart, very smart bird. She thought they loved the bird as much as they would have loved a child. But she didn't know. No one can really know about that.

Wives jumped into the water when their husbands left for sea. I'm no more or less than sand, shell, water, air. So it doesn't make a difference. The man I loved left, after I did. Sometimes I remember his name. Sometimes I don't. It doesn't matter. The weather here. Mild, sunny, diminished with light. Don't believe all they tell you about death. It's lovely and not lovely—lonely, I think, but so light. Swimming in light. Shimmer. I was so happy once. Felt like I didn't deserve it. But I did, even the loss. But what did I lose, lost myself in paint. Chatter of seabirds.

Sometimes she heard birds shouting, clacking, whistling. Saw lights on the horizon at dawn. Boats moored in the harbor as still as all the stones piled in beautiful walls on the island. It was never boring. Ships full of people ready to disappear, moored seven miles away. She could hear them clattering their dishes. Lighting their pipes. Telling their loved ones goodbye.

When did I give up wearing perfume, dearest, pulling a sash around my hair, winding a scarf around my waist? When did I stop caring? When did I remember your name? Something light on the tongue. When will I find my way along the low hills into the birchwood where the sweet translucent berries are all scattered in the bog?

Someone kills a bird here now and then. Someone eats eggs, celery green, the size of my palm. Smashes them on the paths. A kind of reminder of life. How life was, feathers marked in black ink or soft spun fluff. In the grassy beds of winter. Something I can't remember, but someone does. Sadness banished and desire too, just words. Everyone remembers me as nice. Everyone sings the song my sister wrote. Long after her time in the school. That's what I learned today. From someone or other. The pheasant perhaps, or the little gull who sits on the stone wall just outside the window. Not bad to be remembered that way. Even though now this day I can't remember my name. The caretaker and his wife carry boards for their boat. When they get it repaired they're off. Maybe Sweden. Maybe Norway.

It can snow here. Really. After days of pure light. In the graveyard I saw a deep purple crocus. Odd how some things are still funny. The boat that goes away. Comes back with the caretaker and his wife. No one else. Am I the only one on this island? Nothing really matters. But everything does. Elixir. The snowdrops like crushed ice, pure water from the universe.

She told Christine once she loved more than anything to get lost in colors—to take her brush and lose the way—surprise herself. Simple as that. But she's not sure that was true. They were walking home along a street in a city. It was late winter. There were pots of bulbs on the sidewalk. Lanterns with burning candles. Little suns. Now the sun shines right into her face. Her hands don't work. No brushes to paint with here. She can't remember what it's like to make love. Really. No need for that. She's enveloped like a jellyfish in sacred matter. No need to fret, be lonesome, wish for something else. But she remembers it was lovely. Lost in the body of someone else. Suspended like a star. Glitter when it was good.

She used to like to swim in the shallow cove. The water sluicing over her body. Like a mermaid. All surprise, mouth open to the strange taste of air. She loved the smell of water, the taste of salt on her tongue. The way her body disappeared in the tiny ripples of the sea. She won't admit to being bored. But she is. Like when she was sick all those days. Lying in bed. White sheets. White walls, white lights. Now everything is blue. The shimmer of noon on the water. Blue sky, blue sun, blue wings of the seabird. Blue boat, blue cart, blue rope.

Different weather. Yes. Even here that happens. The smell from the mainland. Manure, new grass, salty bay, periwinkle, cloudberry. Something called spring. Clods of chocolate earth. Whose name did I lose first? My own, maybe, into the wind. And then yours, and then yours. Sometimes I wish for deep fog, rough seas and that's what I got today. Though I know just under the thick cold fog there's the celestial blue of the sky. The little seagulls know this too, falling from the sky like confetti. Then darting up. Exhilarated with breaking water. Splitting up on the rocks like milk.

Hirsholm

Simmer Dim

Higher than all mountains
lower than the heather—
a path when walked upon

A bird flying low
blood dripping from its wings—
a boat when rowed

St Ninian's Isle

The woman wears a bone necklace. Long, carved, conveying status. She's rising up out of her grave, hidden under the stones of the church. Long before Christianity on the island and the island is rising up too, shifting off the crofts that made a settlement, with their kale yards and clusters of sheep. Great skuas nest here now and screech over the heads of everyone who walks near their chicks. The woman has long blonde hair and her cloak is ermine, something expensive and rare even then. She's the one who buried five children in their tiny graves and carved a cross on the stones near each head. There were giants here too. You see their stones scattered on the highest places. If you stand on the headland you might be able to see Greenland. Green land, though I doubt you'd be in a hurry to get there. I mistake water for sky, rocks for seals, birds for words, kelp for pudding, plastic for stinging jelly fish, pain for joy, a table for a chessboard, a smile for a grimace, those long dead or forgotten for people I love now, the house for a barrel, prose for a poem, one word for another, a kiss for a bite. Nothing to be done about all this. I was not taught right from wrong.

The Body Is Burden and Delight

The body is burden   and delight
like a yellow pear   perched on the top
of a canister   or your body curled
carefully   around mine
heavy on the sheets   the narrow boats
in the narrow water   full of
boys   their throats open
to the breeze   a child all face
in the carriage   her hat tilted
the movement away   from the body
in conversation   not delight

Just as the mist   comes down
on the girl's   no on the woman's
shoulders   on the clipped grass
of the mountain's   verge
on the muzzle of the sheep   and deep gorge
and gorse   and hawthorn
all more than   the thought
of beauty   she thinks twice
about the top of the mountain   the view from there
the wind from there   the taste of the air
from there

Pools make   themselves known
after the photographer   on the bank
of the silver river   he's always there, my friend tells me
perched on the side   waiting for a beautiful
girl, to take   her picture
in the pool   I slip by him, no longer a girl
but older, as I climb   my limbs slip away, too
nothing left but the rush   of body through bracken, through
gorse and rose and bluebell   little points of sky blue,
pieces of another world   echoing in this

A packet of years   tied in a packet of
slate, like the fences   around and about
these parts   the luscious swoop
of the wagtail   or the swallows
iridescent, beyond the   color of blue
packet of fence posts   packet of
heart strings   invisible from the porch

If you strike your chest   once or twice
and proclaim   the splendor of life
will all things settle   into their rightful
places, the gentle   face of the lamb
the mossy reach of   the branch
the gravel   on the road
the icy green   pool
his house   now yours
his heart   only yours
his daughter and son   now yours
while your first husband   takes the boat
as far   away as he must
(into your arms)

Llanfrothen

Bags of Wool

At first he was the only boy in the village. Seals gathered on the rocks. Large seabirds with black wings flew over his head as he walked to school. His parents had moved from Italy to a place as far away as they could get. The water a shade of blue he'd never seen before. He missed the heat of home. Soon he got used to it. He forgot how to speak to his parents and learned the local dialect, something only people on that island spoke. Something ancient. His mother hummed as she was making his breakfast, his father started weaving beautiful cloth. The bags of wool his dad bought were expensive, but so was the cloth he made his hours at the loom. It was a village of weavers, something that seemed very strange considering it was the twenty-first century. How many people lived in villages anyway? It was like living in a time warp. Soon he wanted to get away. He lived in a cottage and his mother baked, his father wove. It was kind of creepy and he felt like he wanted something different. A kind of flash and pizazz you couldn't find at home. He pierced his ears and met someone who made bracelets out of sheep bones. It didn't matter he couldn't speak Italian. What was language anyway but a bridge from one thought to another. A way to sell goods or get what you wanted. He moved to Glasgow and vowed to not ever step foot in the village again. But here he was, selling his father's beautiful creations to every tourist who came off the boat. It was the summers, he told the woman, the light, the sound of the birds, the snipe with its rattling wings, the silence all night even when the sun was still making a noise. How could he stay away from that?

Vaila Sound

Island Blues

If you round up all the ghosts on the island, there wouldn't be more
      than two, maybe,
the man with a limp prodding his polished cane
              into tufts of grass
the priest from the church whispering to the woman by the blue gate
          I've looked for more, under rocks, by the little cove,
in the garden where the man and his wife burn brush, get things ready
              for summer, birds get themselves ready, too
calling out loudly, standing around, waiting to lay their eggs
               past the lighthouse behind the row of pilot houses
raucous, violent, flashing their black caps and sharp beaks
        the guillemots on the dock just laze the day away
shiny black bodies perched on the edge
            or bobbing in waves, red legs tucked under
ghostly swirls of water, chock-full

2.

Bad things might happen here   but don't
the administrator (face rumpled like a prune)   doesn't kiss me
      though our hips brush
as he changes   the water bottle
(round, plastic   in the pinched room)

   instead   his wife comes back, tall and slim
her suitcase trailing behind her   like a dog

The man with the limp   long dead
born in one of the sloped yellow
          houses
doesn't show up
tapping his cane   on the cobbles

On the mainland   all sorts of things
disappear, crumble   get torn apart
people shoot   don't regret it
a boy (really)   dead on the grass
another blown to bits   gathered by cousins
in Yemen   eating dinner (open air)
          (pale green eggs here   as large as my palm)
not sucked clean, someone else drops them   delicate shells
broken on the path

the big gulls   with blunt beaks
circle my windows   (white feathers blazing)
then disappear   go off to the other island
out of bounds   can't go there (the slender slip of sand)
only the administrator   and his blonde wife, (hair snug against
her neck)

Wives could drown   but they don't
jumping off the dock   when their husbands leave for shore
(my huband waves from the boat   his hand held like a prize
for minutes   as I watch)

(even though everything disappears   into the light)

the sand's cold in the morning on my legs
the tender sea pulling away
from the sandbar like a sheet

3.

You can find amber on the little beach littered   with stones
shy birds
     hang out there
red eyes, red beak, red legs
          perched on two rocks too far away to touch
               the terrible gulls all clustered on the sandbar
(near the forbidden island)
     Germans were here once,
they built bunkers
               so permanent   you'd need big equipment
to break them apart
     water, wind, ice, snow's nothing
but a good thrashing
               even moss won't get a toehold

4.

The caretaker's wife   crouches on the stony beach
               psychedelic lichen plastered on all the rocks
     her back bathed in black   her long slim legs
bathed in black (too)
          the thin hand she uses   to comb silky sand for amber

she's tied her silky hair in a knot (at her neck)
when I lean over   against the sun
                    she looks up
          I saw you walking across the sandbar at dawn
Yes, she says, the forbidden island
               no one goes there except the terrible gulls
               with their sharp curved beaks
               they'll split the necks of other gulls   clean from their bodies
               (leave the feathers in a v on the paths)
                         we crush their eggs

I dig between stones for shells   curved bellies half hidden
          in (crumbled) sand   polished slivers piled up
          wet, shiny
scuff my sneakers in piles of swollen seaweed   I'm not looking
          for amber   hard and golden, centuries old but
breath
          (breath from the animals)
          all gone somewhere else from the shell

                         5.

Oh wicked sun, just a lighthouse
     but so much more insistent, a pool of orange on my lips as I sleep
stung through the still curtain,
          even the seagulls chatter through the night thinking it's day
a flashing sky, the absence of stars
once all these rocks were piled up somewhere else

        along the edges of the island by little coves
rest spots for seals taking sun baths
        I sleep (sort of) on cushions of flowers
odorless, smooth
I don't mind the pulsing of the light,
        stills my heart to sleep

Hirsholm

Light

Deer startled sentinels
      Lean toward the light
All their bristly coats
        Lean toward the light
Green now after rain,
      Leans toward light
Leans toward the river of light
        A pool compressed on the lawn, leans
Toward the light
          Everyone's there   the shiny fox leans
Into light
      Her kits one and then two
A clapping
        Of light
Jagged once or twice and then thunder, all the brushy woods
      Electric with light and
         rain drops as big as plums lean to light
The water below me in the brook tumbles
      and leans
          All light after rain, soft and wide
All growing things confident and blessed after rain   lean toward
      Light, the little hawks startled with song,
        Light leaning perched on the raggy tree,
A whole family scooping up the wonder of it
      (lightly) leaning

Brownsville

Quince

In the garden two young women
are pulling strands of black out of the pond

I'm on the porch of a house as old as I am
but much more beautiful, built in the Japanese style,

it's all sun and wood and calm as I stand watching the women
work to clean the pond,

one bends her head over the water, her long blonde hair
dips across her face, the other

stands on the little bank, her black hair pulled in a knot at her neck—
soon, a young man appears with a mower to trim Turtle Island

a place of great good luck
the stream tumbles down rough rocks pooling here and there

near the bath house,
where a wooden bathtub stands empty and small

I've spotted a quince bush unfurling new leaves like tiny ears
after the bright blossom has dropped,

there's a stone basin to dip my hands in and a bamboo dipper
I move from one room to another in my socks,

the tatami mats slightly warm
under my toes

Shofuso

The Path at Llanfrothen

At the flat the wagtail   chirps
wet grass   sweet in the mist
cold stove
a sweep of landscape   filled with
the river   of brown cows
moving in and   out
of the field   upstairs Pia
marks her papers   silver
sheets of   rain
wet   my hair

On the lane   the woodpecker
spatters the air with   notes
scaring me off
her noisy   nestlings
little beaks in the   hollowed
circle   of the wood

This is the house where   Irene lives
new paint for the wedding   cream and rose
this is the house   where Brian lives
moving his sheep   and cows
from one field to the next   sometimes borrowed
this is the   house
where another woman   once lived
and met the farmer down   the hill
in the field at night   and day
or deep in the morning

I walk through bracken in   the hollow
past the brook where   Irene dips in the morning
like a figure in a painting   all white against
dark green oaks and mossy   rocks
and then up   the road
to Ogoronwy   and through the pasture past
Nia's house and the empty   chapel
across the thick slate   bridge past Plas
under the pink full   rose to the old church
Nia meets me near the bridge   her hair streaked with gray
her dog placing   log after log
on the grass   for her to throw

(And into your arms)

The Italian Mystery

1.

In the Italian mystery there is a knife and a lake. The lake is bordered by fluffy trees. Once the knife was a kitchen knife, quiet in its drawer. I saw the knife in a plastic bag, enveloped in mist. No, that was the lake, and the heroine was standing by the lake where her mother killed her father. Such family drama. Once there was a family and then there was none. Just the calm water of the lake, the reflection of the trees, the mother opening her mouth to speak and the daughter starting to cry. But this was a long time ago in another world, minus the father who was long dead. And the mother who decided she didn't like how the story was going and got out of town fast.

2.

Once he kept telling her he wanted it doggie style. He told her this over and over again. There were cardinals in the bushes by the canal. She could hear them whistling to each other. She could see their fiery heads. In the paper the reviewer said violent sex was the best, full of heat and love. The book he was discussing had lots of it. Chains and whips, humiliation. Giving yourself completely over to the other. She didn't think that sounded like fun. To let yourself go in pain was the last thing she wanted. But it was fashionable then on the lip of the new decade. You had to include it somewhere or no one would read your work.

3.

It was all about how once upon a time there were keys to the house. Held fast in her mother's hands. There was her mother on the deck leaning out toward the big maple. Deer put their delicate hooves into the wet soil under the tree. You can see them there even now. The dust of insects. A pair of reindeer shoes eaten invisible by northern bugs. The sound of her brother and sister whining that the house was falling down, the carpenter refused to work. The lights in the fir trees must mean something was going on. Surely someone would want to buy such a house and wipe away the mirage of a family who was happy in its skin.

4.

Once there were fires burning everywhere. In my heart. In suburban backyards. Koalas drinking from tubs under frothy bushes. Grief displayed like art hung in the trees. A forest with ghosts like the one on the flank of Fuji. Meanwhile minor terror reigned over the land. Not enough to destroy the world but on its way. The sick barricaded on cruise ships. Their laundry flying from balconies. The forsythia out too early, too early for spring. And where was winter? Hiding in the bushes, asleep at the wheel, looking out for itself. I had seen many winters. The far shore leaping up all of a sudden to claim me.

5.

Once upon a time my grandmother washed the jalousies on the porch. I got them all done, Cherie. Whew, it was quite a job. I could smell the ammonia and liked the way the slats glistened. It was warm there, as warm as the hall in winter when I would curl up on the floor near the hot air vent and sleep. My grandfather did the same thing on the floor in the living room at the base of the couch. She was French. He was Irish. There was a shiny pamphlet full of beautiful women with bare breasts in the drawers upstairs. My grandparents had visited Paris. The Folies Bergere. Could I have breasts like that some day? Could I wind leaves around my body and fold my neck back to let all the world see my beautiful breasts?

6.

The birds look at me with suspicion. So suspiciously. Glass eyes long beaks. Once they were in a shop here and there. Why aren't they happy? I've liberated them from the sticky hands of children, the sweaty hands of mothers. Ungrateful birds. Caricatures of their real cousins who throw stones off high cliffs in northern places or steal through the bush and call out at night to their mates or pose on the wires above the inlet where godwits poke their beaks into the muck and fur seals tumble near the road while three women from Singapore snap picture after picture and cry out in glee.

Owl-light

*In the darkness an eye stares
showing others the way—
the moonlight revealing
a road for friends*

Snow

The man she could have loved
the man she once loved
spare of face and body
the man she wanted to love
spare of face and body
the flat pool above his house
bordered with split stone
a mountain full of snow
a forest full of their
footsteps
wedged in furrows
the tumbling brook
wracked with limbs
the tumbling stream
of ticking years
on the face, the long thin face
of the man she wanted to love
his house,
the thin white house
his hands, his arms
his lips
on the lips of another woman
spare of face and body
in the town far away
from the white house, near
the white horse with heavy head bent
to the pond
lost in the past,
near the mountain white now
with snow

Ogoronwy

Letter

Is the daughter married
                    (The squirrel just stole a tomato)
The fifth lamb born
                          (Green and round)
            The stove repaired
                                                Soon to warm
Cows threading their way in the sculpted field

His anger quelled
                          The stream icy cold
Your heart well worn
                          (The squirrel is in the tree)
            Your son on the boat
                  In the bay
Your daughter in the ancient town
                          The first-year lambs shorn
Woodpeckers fledged
                          Pia's garden weeded
New owners in the shop
                          Armed with those delicious date cakes
The songs all sung
                                (About the miners)
Caves empty of bats
            Owl spit on the foxglove
His grandchildren playing in the square with
                                (All their new friends)
The song of the wagtail vibrant
                          Roses in bloom
(Once again)

Imitating Celestial Things

Blazing bitternut hickory, kingfishers darting up down the river ten
miles or so out of town, a week later, gone (dry smell after a

liquid world) once the river was high and brown racing along in
glinting sun (once hickories) "crunched green nut husks to

poison fish for food" the wood good for burning, good for barrel
hoops and skis, wagons, gunstocks, chair backs and baskets

other apparitions, puffball mushrooms on the ball field, praying
mantis, cicada carcasses, a shiny spider with brown legs poised

in her huge web, strung from umbrella to door
(here and then gone, liquid quiver of the earthquake)

I've been thinking about turtles and the river, (silky wide river),
two hundred years ago you could see the water from where I sit

(a couple of weeks ago I was walking by the river)
north to the little hills called the Blue

Mountains, a woman holding something like a small camera
(when I got close enough) I saw it was a turtle

the turtle on my palm, her smooth yellow plastron, cool and hard
(she stuck her head out, green)

streaked neck, amber eyes, legs popping from the shell, soon she
was running all the way to high rough water under the bridge

she walks on the bottom of the river, avoids swift currents (the map
turtle doesn't leave) the water except to sunbathe or lay eggs,

she hibernates in deep slow water, (sometimes) if the frozen river's
transparent, you can see turtles move under the ice

Down the street a cauldron of tar cooking, roofers stir with big
sticks (evening primrose along the river, goldfinches chatter)

geese root around in grass along the riverbank
near empty concrete pads where

there used to be picnic tables (a bloody tampon almost hidden) in
bushes along restored walks of the nineteenth century

waterworks, a broad winged hawk calls out now and then (my son
has two weeks before he leaves for college)

an Eastern carpenter bee lives in the lattice on the deck, throwing
sawdust into a little pile, a miniature dune (she excavates

tunnels for her brood) encased there, snug in the wood
"Adults emerge in late summer, each

waiting in line toward
the end of the tunnel for its turn to leave"

(Snipping bodies of tulips, creamy yellow streaked with red flames)
I've been reading about Japan, obsessed with stories of

hidden mountains and flat shimmering rice paddies glowing against
the horizon (I'm not sure what's real), several writers tell me people

in Japan can see only what they want to see in the landscape
the cherry tree against a white sky and not concrete pilings in

the distance, ancient firs bent
at the edge of the garden and not the pachinko parlor

Snowdrops open their wings in the little garden
bed, the mockingbird sits on a fat, scraggly bush singing all sorts

of songs, warming up for the big concert, icebergs on the sidewalk
behind CVS (I took a look at them yesterday) thinking this is how

the Arctic must be melting, from the bottom up, water seeping out
from under hunks of ice and flowing down the drain into the river

Iris reticulata, deep blue (almost as blue as mountain gentians)
blooms along the side of the house, the garden as balance in the

city "between artifice and nature, between war and peace, between
health and disease" Giovanni Leoni in his essay about sixteenth

century Ferrara in The Italian Garden tells the story of gardens
that circled city walls (the duke could walk all the way around),

hidden by the series of artificial landscapes, he could sneak someone
dangerous or important into the castle protected by gardens

(the garden a magical ring around the city) Leoni writes the linked
gardens could capture "the stars by imitating celestial things"

Yesterday the Dalai Lama was on the Today Show, Ann Curry
interviewed him, I was sipping coffee, standing in the living room

with my mother, "He's really old, isn't he?" my mother asked (I said),
"Oh, not so old, look at his hands, they look young"

Ann Curry repeated everything the Dalai Lama said for a while, and
then gave up (he's the kind of person you would

want to tell) all your troubles to,
he told her we're more compassionate,

smarter than we've ever been,
don't worry, the universe is a very old place

One of my mother's neighbors keeps beehives, "Styrofoam, everything's plastic now"

he showed me the little box the queen comes in (tiny wooden container with wire inserts and a plug at the end) "Some people

just let her chew her way out, but I pop the plug after a couple of hours"

bees just disappear, the queen may still be alive but no workers clean the cells or fan the air or feed larvae or

guard the hive entrance, no bees gather pollen and bring it back to the hive

Scientists implant transmitters in bar-tailed godwits, they fly distances of 7,100 miles nonstop (Arctic terns fly from

Greenland to South America or the farthest tip of Africa), scooping up fish from the Atlantic on the way

A man who grows strawberries near here for a little extra cash shot seven cedar waxwings and a chipping sparrow (eating his fruit, he

said, and it's part of his livelihood) I've seen cedar waxwings in a bog where they nest (tiny fledglings as miraculous as their parents)

soft gray, a splash of yellow, spots of red and a jaunty crest (they're common birds, the shooter said)

I had to look up a chipping sparrow, their song is the sweetest of the spring songs

I fell in love with a painting, in spring after a long winter (but first I fell in love with Japan) the first green of spring

you feel it in the painting, dried grasses of fall, a small sound at the margin, snow and dark branches of winter giving way to the blush

of green on the edges of the canvas, the idea of a path, and a frozen pool (a mirror of something I didn't know about)

I'd been reading about Japan in *Sakuteiki, Visions of the Japanese Garden*, a translation of one of the oldest books on gardening or

"the art of setting stones"
stones were alive and the gardener had to listen to their desires,

the book was written on two long scrolls in the late eleventh century about the gardens of Kyoto just after it was built,

springs, brooks, waterfalls, and ponds
"The garden was envisioned as a conglomerate of

'vignettes' of the natural world" the writer of *Sakuteiki* directed the gardener to "select several places within the property according to

the shape of land and ponds and create a subtle atmosphere, reflecting again and again on one's memories of wild nature"

Today I learned what deixis is, a pronoun demanding attention,
"a contextual speech act" I heard a poet speak about the poem as

entrapment, stopping traffic to cross the street through banks of
twilight snow, a tree I never noticed demanding I touch a

branch or run my finger along her twig, the squirrel's nest on
campus, too, speaks to me, cold moving into my throat like dust

Last night I dreamed I was pulling my mother through the
ocean, the waves were blue–gray, and I held her hand as we

were tossed around in icy water and then felt sand under my
toes, I pulled as hard as I could to get us to land,

but the cold waves just kept pushing back
against us

Everyone's seen the wall of oily water going 500 miles an hour,
(beaches filled with disaster) Alex Kerr in his book *Dogs and*

Demons writes of the Japanese love of concrete
rivers and oceans walled off, controlled, now the country's moved

eight feet and the globe's rotation sped up
(or slowed down), "time" displaced

Kazumi Saeki in his essay in *The New York Times* this morning
writes, "The fierce rolling of the earth lasted longer than I had

ever experienced" (he drove home from an inn to his house near
the ocean) "When I looked out toward the ocean the next morning,

I saw in horror that neighborhoods close to the sea
had simply vanished

Now an invisible pollution is beginning to spread, people have
acquired a desire for technology that surpasses human

comprehension, yet the bill that has come due for that
desire is all too dear"

Tohoku

Late Snow

The man's on the shed, nailing down corrugated metal
        deadly in this wind

        wind on the spores of moss, the loopy line of trees, on sodden
dangerous grass,

his wife, not really a farmer's wife
                watched him from the doorway of a caravan

    where dolls hide
(I know they're in there somewhere)

I mop the damp that seeps under the slate in the
                        kitchen,

        a fire, the wind, the rain,
fiery moss curled on

        wet stone, a garden just
there, beyond the window

        an exclamation of the beauty of
this singular world

                fit in the valley
below the mountain,

        (like a knight's hat)
pointed, slowly,

slippery at the top

dangerous,
        for two hikers,
with no water, no food

small details that
        amuse me now

                sitting in front of the fire
                        that wants

a log

Croesor

When the Child Was Born

When the child was born that was good news
when the lemon was sweet like an orange

and the priest cupped his hands on the chalice
that was good news, when the little boy

ran through the grass and his father
scooped him up when the wind blew

that was good news, when the iris bloomed
in snow dark blue and burning like a lemon

that was good news, and when the mother
touched her son's cheek, soft and warm

and the trees in the pine wood sighed
that was good news, the rabbit hunched

on the side of the wood brown and soft
ears twitching hawks tumbling

in the brittle cold sky,
when the stone washed up on the shore

that was good news,
when the cup was hot with tea

the sparrows fluffed out in the cold
the raisin sweet on the tongue

that was good news

In the Shed

Alder burns hot even when new
   young lambs okay with warm milk even in snow
snow now when I wake after hours of sleep
    wind strong
new lambs still brown with blood—their mother licking them
        clean as one nurses
colostrum in the stomach—put in through a tube—
      nutrients to get them off to a good start—

Some farmers put plastic coats on newborn lambs—
      warmth in this unseasonable cold
better safe than sorry—Brian says
    Irene carefully folding a wet sweater into a towel—
coffee in a china cup—like a fairy's breakfast
      kitchen=fire

Walking through dusk, mountains above us
     sheep following to the pony's hut—
  basket of hay put so wind won't blow it
      away—hollows of grass filled with snow
air/light/wind breaking up like matter
    spots of the world exchanging place so everything's
split apart, tinged with a kind of
    elemental no color, no world, no time, no
shimmery water

Sun breaks on the camellias, freezing cold—

    the sheep calling out as Brian feeds them in the shed—

I know a new lamb's there—licked clean

    by her mother who gave birth in the corner, the

other sheep turned away

Llanfrothen

The Forest Near Paneriai

1.

Vilnius was the last place she wanted to be. She distrusted its beautiful streets winding past courtyards full of cars and cats and huddled ghosts, its beautiful flowers wrapped in tight bundles for sale on wide boulevards, the crumbling church at the prison, the shallow river that ran through the park. Even the flocks of swallows seemed to be telling her something important about her life so far. Everywhere she looked there was something significant going on, a man touching a woman's lips with his thumb. A woman unfurling an umbrella when there was no rain in sight. Little children played instruments of different types along the busiest street where tourists arrived in busloads and trainloads from all over. Minsk, Wisconsin, Japan. And who was she in the middle of all this choreographed confusion, but a woman, on the verge of being old, bundled into herself, wondering about her child now grown, her husband solicitous, her memories washed away like the dirt, poured down sloping streets to the river in the park.

2.

Vilnius was the last place she wanted to be. Her cat talking to her by the geraniums, thirsty at the door. The narrow man who lived with his mother in the next apartment beating his rug on the line as she watched from the window. Dust flying up into the air in clouds, covering the little white dog from next door, butterflies in the bush on the edge of the wild grass, her fingernails as she poured water for the cat, the perfect flowers of the hollyhock. He beat the striped red rug and then brushed it with several swift downward sweeps and then beat the rug and brushed it again and again until there was hardly any dust in the air at all.

3.

Vilnius was the last place she wanted to be. But there it was. The coffee in her hand that morning, the sound of trucks coming up the hill past the apartment. The empty square where Lenin used to stand. The empty woods where her grandmother was shot. She was lucky to be here at all and wouldn't be, would she, if her mother hadn't been lucky enough to walk one morning out of the ghetto down the hill to the park and into another life. It was a kind of miracle, something she didn't like to think about but had to now and then. Soon she wouldn't be here at all, but somewhere else. Nevada, Vermont, Philadelphia.

4.

Vilnius was the last place she wanted to be. A city in the middle of woods. She could never get warm even when he lit all the lamps and stuffed the stove with wood and rubbed her feet with his hands. She was eating beautiful red berries her child picked in the woods and mushrooms curled and yellow her husband sold in the market. She was eating quail eggs scrambled in a wide pan. She was eating all the bounty of the forest but was still hungry. It was strange this went on for so long in such a city so filled with balconies filigreed, delicate, hung on the sides of buildings with such skill.

5.

Vilnius was the last place she wanted to be. She thought she was telling herself the truth when she said that, when she told the stranger sitting on the hard bench at the airport that kind of thing. She thought it was certainly true as she poured water into her cup, or picked up a bunch of bananas in the market, or swallowed the first sip of tea, or petted the coarse hair of the little white dog who lived in the beautiful courtyard. Someone was vacuuming on a Sunday. It was early but there were no bells ringing. It was unusual to be in such a holy city and not hear bells ring on Sunday morning. Someone had cut the grass in the courtyard and the white butterflies had all vanished. So much had disappeared. Sometimes the tree by the window was full of birds, and sometimes there was no sound at all. A plane flew overhead. The flight path must have changed, she thought. She had never heard an airplane here before.

6.

The sky was shot through with clouds. Every day, since she arrived, the sky was pure blue. Innocent, benign, all those words that meant one is not responsible for anything. Not anything at all. She, certainly, was not one to blame, even if this and that had happened and now women with sheer apricot and green dresses stepped lightly on the streets.

Water

When she looked at the word she couldn't
remember what it meant—something
to do with the past or a cup or wet toes—
things were missing—voices, wind, boards on
the sides of houses, her son's brush. In a
short story someone—the young
wife—died, her daughter fed pigeons, her
father slept. Sometimes she was
sure she knew where it was. Perhaps
under her bed, behind the curtain,
in the hollow under her fingernails, she
was determined she would not hear
the thud of her heart as she slept or
feel the steady quick rhythm of her
pulse against her finger.
Somewhere there was
a man fishing in a cold river in the
far north. She knew who he
was, she was sure soon he would
flick his line into the river and
touch water.

Deatnu

Notes

"Higher Than All Mountains " is a traditional Sámi song translated by Harald Gaski and Mari Boine on her album, *Bálvvoslatjna—Room of Worship* (1998).

Emma Ricklund (1897-1965) was a Swedish artist and innkeeper who encouraged fellow artists and displayed their work in her hotel in northern Sweden.

Emilie Demant Hatt (1873-1958): Danish artist, writer, and ethnographer worked with Sámi artist and writer Johan Turi in writing and translating *An Account of the Sámi*.

In his book *Vilnius: City of Strangers*, Laimonas Briedis writes, "A vast majority of the Vilne Jews were killed by Germans and Lithuanian collaborators in Ponary (Paneriai), the forested hill overlooking the city where the Napeolonic Army met its end in 1812. The ghetto was liquidated on September 23, 1943, with most of its eleven thousand remaining inhabitants sent to concentration camps in Estonia, where few survived the hard labour and starvation. Out of sixty thousand local Jews, no more than three thousand survived the end of the war" (227). See Briedis, *Vilnius: City of Strangers*. Central European University Press, 2009.

Acknowledgments

Gratefully acknowledged are the following publications, where particular poems appeared previously in different forms:

Ecozona ("Spring Migration, " "What You Do, " "Everything is Liquid," "If There's a Woman There's a Dish")

Western Humanities Review ("Island Blues 1")

Devouring the Green ("Island Blues 2-5")

ISLE ("Light and "Imitating Celestial Things")

DIAGRAM ("The Italian Mystery")

Cloudbank ("When the Child Was Born")

Green Mountains Review ("The Forest Near Paneriai")
    *winner of the Neil Shepard Prize for Fiction

Special thanks to Ricklundgarden in Saxnas, Sweden; Brecht's House in Svendborg, Denmark; The Council of Danish Artists, Hirsholmene, Denmark; Creator in Residence, Hillswick, Shetland; along with the Caselberg Trust, New Zealand, for residencies; and a fellowship from the Summer Literary Seminars, Vilnius, Lithuania. And thank you to Harald Gaski for permission to use his translation of "Higher Than All Mountains."

Many thanks to Temple University for a sabbatical to live and travel in Denmark.

I'm grateful to Karen Donovan and Elaine Terranova who guided this book through many drafts.

Thank you to Dr. Ross Tangedal, Grace Dahl, Brett Hill, Julia Kaufman, and Korah Jacob at Cornerstone Press for their attentive work and good cheer.

Awel Irene has often given me a place to write and welcomed me into her home in Wales. A huge thank you.

A warm thanks to Mette von Buchwald, my friend and walking buddy in Denmark.

Scott and Graham Masker have been my intrepid companions on many of these journeys.

SHARON WHITE is an author, poet, and educator. Her book *Vanished Gardens: Finding Nature in Philadelphia* won the Association of Writers and Writing Programs award in creative nonfiction. *Boiling Lake (On Voyage)*, a collection of short fiction, is her most recent work. She is also the author of two collections of poetry, *Eve & Her Apple* and *Bone House*.

Her memoir, *Field Notes, A Geography of Mourning*, received the Julia Ward Howe Prize, Honorable Mention, from the Boston Authors Club. Some of her other awards include the Marguerite McGlinn Prize for Fiction from Philadelphia Stories, the Neil Shepard Prize from Green Mountains Review, Italo Calvino Prize in Fabulist Fiction, a Pennsylvania Council on the Arts Fellowship for Creative Nonfiction, the Leeway Foundation Award for Achievement, a Colorado Council on the Arts Fellowship, and a National Endowment for the Arts Fellowship. Sharon is an Associate Professor Emerita at Temple University.